Beyond 'Ah-Ha'

52 powerful ways to start challenging life's rules

BRONWEN SCIORTINO

COVER DESIGN: Book Baby LLC
www.bookbaby.com

COVER & INTERNAL IMAGE: Lorelei Ammon
www.ammonart.com.au; facebook.com/loreleiammonartist

TYPESETTING: Kelsey Allen, Media Highway
www.mediahighway.com.au

ISBN 978-0-9943188-6-2 (hardcover)

Sciortino, Bronwen

Beyond 'Ah-Ha' (52 Powerful Ways to Start Challenging Life's Rules)

Includes Index

OTHER RESOURCES:
Access free resources from bronwensciortino.com:
• bronwensciortino.com/7-steps-to-living-differently-email-series/
• bronwensciortino.com/free-tools/

FOLLOW BRONWEN SCIORTINO:

FACEBOOK
www.facebook.com/bronwensciortinoauthor

INSTAGRAM
www.instagram.com/bronwensciortino_author

LINKEDIN
www.linkedin.com/in/bronwensciortino

WEBSITE
www.bronwensciortino.com

CONTACT
Email: info@sheiqlife.com
Phone: +61 438 624 868

ABOUT THE AUTHOR

Bronwen Sciortino is an internationally renowned Author, Simplicity Expert and Professional Speaker who spent almost two decades as a high-achieving, award-winning executive before experiencing a life-changing event that forced her to stop and ask the question "What if there's a better way to live?"

Based in Perth, Western Australia, Bronwen works with people globally through corporate programs, conference platforms, retreats, professional mentoring and in the online environment. She shares her secrets to living life differently, inspires individuals to simplify their lives and helps them to embrace the concept of an economy of enough.

Bronwen is a part of the exclusive Talent Concierge team of global speakers, blogs regularly for global platforms, has been featured in 'The Book of Amazing People', 'Reboot Your Life – Phoenix Edition', and 'Successful Women in Business – Winners Edition', and is regularly invited as a guest on blogs, podcasts and member sites throughout the world.

In her spare time, you'll find Bronwen on her yoga mat, immersed in the world of meditation, curled up with a great book, hanging with her husband and cat or exploring the great outdoors.

DEDICATION

For all who seek their absolute truth ...
may this book guide you home to complete happiness.

Much love

Bron xo

CONTENTS

INTRODUCTION

Life is spinning at a greater speed than ever before and it's easy to be distracted by people, places and things that mean very little to you. You can find yourself being pulled in all different directions at the same time – and let's be honest, that's exhausting. There's often so much happening that you can't remember what happened yesterday, let alone weeks, months or years ago.

Living like this, and looking around at everyone else seemingly succeed, can leave you wondering what you are doing with your life. And it's not a nice feeling.

Recent years have seen the rise of the 'Ah-Ha' moment. It's become 'the' thing that you have to chase so you can be free from the prison that life has become. But with each 'Ah-Ha' moment comes a moment of truth – a moment that shows you how and why your life hasn't lived up to that 'Ah-Ha' to date.

The truth can be terrifying because with it comes the need for change, and when change is required age-old conditioning kicks in – suddenly it all seems very hard. So, even though you've done what you were supposed to and you've found your 'Ah-Ha', you're suddenly stuck with a piece of information that 'should be' life changing … but you don't know what to do with it.

Being stuck with your 'Ah-Ha' can be daunting and often leads to complete overwhelm. One of the most powerful tools I created when I was rebooting my own life was to develop an easy way to find MY own answers. After quite a bit of trial and error, I found that the easiest way was to find the questions that allowed me to decide what I wanted – and didn't want – to experience every day.

Often your greatest challenge is to overcome and quieten your mind. It's almost always your mind that steps in to stop you from making any significant change in your life. So, maybe stop trying to fight the power of your mind and instead harness it and put it work.

One of the easiest ways to do this is to start asking yourself questions.

Not just any questions – but questions that matter. Questions that help you to consciously find your own answers. Questions that can help to release the hold that auto-pilot has on your life, and that will allow you to consciously make decisions about what step you would like to take next.

Questions carry the power to reconnect you with your own soul.

Beyond 'Ah-Ha' has been designed to help you to start challenging the rules that your auto-pilot has placed around your life. It contains fifty two questions that you can use to discover more about yourself and the life you truly desire. Ask the questions in order, one week at a time, for all fifty-two weeks of the year … or open at random and trust that the question you land on is the question you need the most in that moment.

Allow your mind to go where it wants to when exploring each question and then let YOUR answers flow.

Remember: there are no right or wrong answers; whatever comes up for you is perfect. As the answers come, allow yourself to see them with empathy and to view them as small pieces of information that will reconnect you with your inner truth.

Embrace the *'Ah-Ha'* moments that come to you as part of this process and never be afraid of your truth – it's not something to be feared and it needs no explanation. Look at your truth through eyes that are filled with self-compassion and allow your truth to be interesting rather than confronting.

As you let your answers flow, try to see the words as a set of information that has formed on your page. That information will give you your next set of questions and the answers will help you shape your next step.

Your truth is waiting for you to catch up and embrace it. Let your mind open and reveal the truth of you that is waiting inside. The more you allow your truth to stand in the light of day, the more you will understand about yourself and the more you will come to see the greatness that you have been hiding from the world.

Life can be so simple, when you let it be so.

This book has been written to help you find a stronger connection with who you really are. May you delight in the depths of your truth and may your answers help you find your way home.

YOUR JOURNALING JOURNEY

Journaling is one of those activities that divides the world. Yes, you're a unique individual, with unique experiences, but there are also some commonalities that can be seen in the way you interact in the world. Journaling is no different, and you will usually align with one of the following three groups:

- **You love it.** It drives you every day and you can't wait to see what comes from the time you spend letting your words flow onto the page.

- **You loathe it.** The mere thought terrifies you and you can't understand why you would want your words out in the open where others might find them.

- **You think it might be something you'd like to try.** You've heard it's a great process for clearing your mind and finding clarity … but you have no idea how to start.

There is no 'right' or 'wrong' in where you fit; some of you might even find that you cross over between two of the groups above. Wherever you are is absolutely perfect for you, right now.

For too long, the world has taught you that you're not good enough – that there are things about yourself that you need to change. You've been told that you have to be stressed to be successful and that if you're not busy then you're not working hard enough.

Beyond 'Ah-Ha' has been written in a way to help you, no matter which group you fit into. Its purpose is to help you find your truth, to welcome the information it brings you with open and loving arms and then to use that information to help you navigate your way forward in a kinder and more gentle way.

I'm often asked how you can start to live life differently. My answer is always that you start by learning how to learn from yourself. By this I mean put some processes in place that help you to do the following:

- **Empower:** understand what is it that you need to be empowered in your own life.

- **Simple:** find the ways that you can give yourself what you need in the simplest and kindest way possible.

- **Connection:** remember who you are and make sure you are consciously connected with what you need.

Remember all of those things you learned as you were growing up? Like all the things you were told were 'right' and 'wrong', 'good' and 'bad', 'acceptable' and 'not'? And all the things that you 'have to do' and 'can't possibly do' and what 'you're capable of' and what is 'beyond you'? Coupled with the ever increasing speed of life, it's little wonder you're so disconnected with who you are and desperately grasping at straws to try and get back on track.

Beyond 'Ah-Ha' gives you the opportunity to reconnect with who you truly are, through asking yourself some simple questions. Answering each of the questions allows you to gain insight into where you are at right now, and then gives you the tools to work out where you would like to go next.

Instead of being judgemental, harsh or critical about an 'Ah-Ha' that comes to you, allow yourself the privilege of having an enquiring mind. Where you are right now isn't as important as where you are going – nor is how you got yourself there as important as how you might like to get yourself somewhere else.

Sometimes it can be hard to get the journaling process started, so I've made it easier for you by including questions that can get your thoughts going.

This is your time to explore and reconnect with who you are. Use it in the way that best serves who you are and what you need.

Enjoy your journey – may it bring you everything you need in exactly the right moment.

With love,

Bron x

1

If today could start with a blank page, what story would you write?

– Bronwen Sciortino

What story will you write today?

You are the most talented and creative of story tellers – but you don't know it. You weave your magic in a complex and beautiful way – yet you are unaware. You are the mastermind behind the story that is your life. In every choice you bring consciousness to what happens; you create the path in front of you.

It is time. Wake and emerge with the greatest of ease and grace. Take control of the story and guide it in all the ways that bring you joy, happiness, love and laughter. Take a blank page and write the story that you always dreamed could be yours.

What were your first thoughts when reading this quote and considering this question?
How did the question and quote make you feel?
Where has this shown up as a pattern in your life?

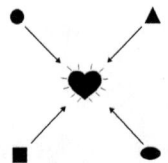

How are you grateful for your experience with this so far?

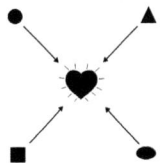

What do you wish was true for you here?
What is your 'Ah-Ha' moment here?

Are there things you need to do differently?
What are they, and what are three things you can do to make them happen?

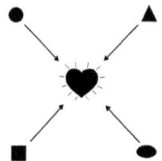

Other thoughts?

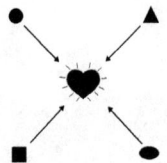

2

Do you remember who you were before the world told you who you should be?

– Danielle LaPorte

Who will you be today?

From the time you were little, there have been so many influences telling you who you 'should' be. Over time, you morph and change yourself so that you fit the mould of the person you think the world is telling you to be. Along the way, you forgot to be who you truly are. At the very heart of it, there are two questions that drive your life: 'Who am I?' and 'Why am I here?'

You're probably lost when trying to answer either of these questions. So, make it easier on yourself by focusing on just one of them. Who are you? What is at the heart of your character?

What were your first thoughts when reading this quote and considering this question?

How did the question and quote make you feel?

Where has this shown up as a pattern in your life?

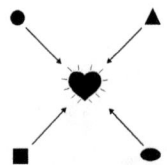

How are you grateful for your experience with this so far?

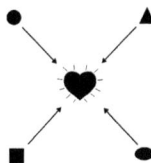

What do you wish was true for you here?
What is your 'Ah-Ha' moment here?

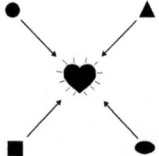

Are there things you need to do differently?
What are they, and what are three things you can do to make them happen?

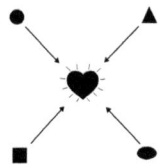

Other thoughts?

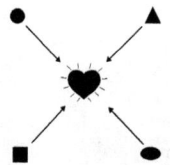

3

What happens when you fear change more than you fear death?

– Bronwen Sciortino

How will you embrace change today?

Change. It's a word that can strike fear in your heart. You've been taught that change is too hard, so now you don't even try. Your life isn't working for you but you can't seem to find a way to do things differently.

You've followed the trends, you've read all the books – and they've dumped you in a place where your life is stuck. What if change was simply a sign that there's a different way for you to live? What if change can actually lead you to the path that was always meant to be yours?

Would that allow you to embrace change and make it your friend?

What were your first thoughts when reading this quote and considering this question?

How did the question and quote make you feel?

Where has this shown up as a pattern in your life?

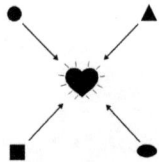

How are you grateful for your experience with this so far?

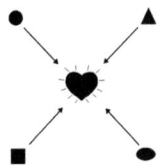

What do you wish was true for you here?
What is your 'Ah-Ha' moment here?

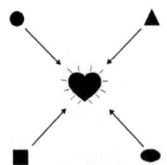

Are there things you need to do differently?
What are they, and what are three things you can do to make them happen?

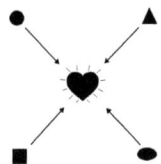

Other thoughts?

4

The most important thing is honouring where you are right now.

How will you honour where you are now?

Wherever you find yourself right now is absolutely perfect. You can spend an incredible amount of time worrying about all the things that are wrong with you – your life, your job, your relationships, your fitness, your finances (and the list goes on). Step into the simplicity of making peace with where you are right now. Once you're at peace with where you are, you can work out what your next step is to take you forward.

Every new day offers you the opportunity to make peace with where you are, and then take your next step into a wide and wondrous world.

What were your first thoughts when reading this quote and considering this question?

How did the question and quote make you feel?

Where has this shown up as a pattern in your life?

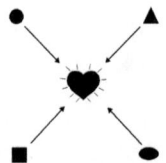

How are you grateful for your experience with this so far?

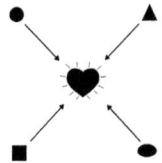

What do you wish was true for you here?
What is your 'Ah-Ha' moment here?

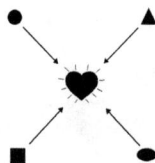

Are there things you need to do differently?
What are they, and what are three things you can do to make them happen?

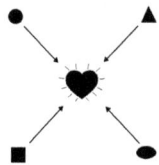

Other thoughts?

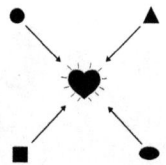

5

Need to detox from your day? Get outside!

– Bronwen Sciortino

How will you detox from your day?

It can feel like the weight of the world is sitting heavily on your shoulders. You run around after everyone else, giving so much more than you allow yourself to receive. Sometimes, it can be hard to recognise when you are in the middle of these situations.

So, it can be handy to create a regular ritual that helps you to detox from your day. As often as you can, get outside and, if possible, stand next to a tree. Spend a few minutes breathing deeply and on every exhale, imagine the toxic load simply melting away with the breath.

What were your first thoughts when reading this quote and considering this question?
How did the question and quote make you feel?
Where has this shown up as a pattern in your life?

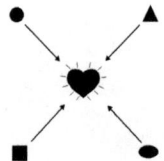

How are you grateful for your experience with this so far?

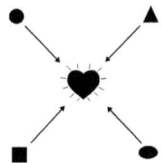

What do you wish was true for you here?
What is your 'Ah-Ha' moment here?

Are there things you need to do differently?
What are they, and what are three things you can do to make them happen?

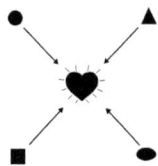

Other thoughts?

6

What if every thought started with love?

– Bronwen Sciortino

What if every thought started with love?

So often life teaches you to start your thought process from a place of judgement. You see someone doing or saying something and you immediately make a decision about whether that is right or wrong.

What if instead, you could see the behaviour or what is being said as an opportunity to simply identify the things that you align to, and those that you don't? This gives you the ability to separate the person from the behaviour and to allow everyone the opportunity to be themselves in every interaction.

What were your first thoughts when reading this quote and considering this question?
How did the question and quote make you feel?
Where has this shown up as a pattern in your life?

How are you grateful for your experience with this so far?

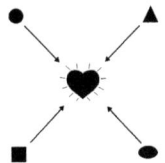

What do you wish was true for you here?
What is your 'Ah-Ha' moment here?

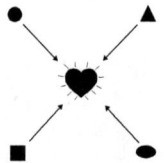

Are there things you need to do differently?
What are they, and what are three things you can do to make them happen?

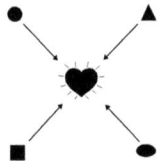

Other thoughts?

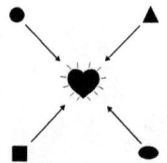

7

Make every situation a win-win where the first win is yours.

– Bronwen Sciortino

How will you ensure that the first 'win' is yours?

You've been taught that it is selfish to think of yourself. So many times in life you find yourself in situations where someone else has all the gains, and you give everything you have. It's no wonder that more and more often you feel exhausted – like you have very little left to give.

If you are always in situations where you are giving, then you are never receiving. When you don't receive you can't experience the joy of refuelling your energy. Start looking for the opportunities where you benefit from the exchange as well, and then allow yourself the joy that winning brings.

What were your first thoughts when reading this quote and considering this question?
How did the question and quote make you feel?
Where has this shown up as a pattern in your life?

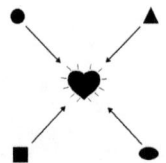

How are you grateful for your experience with this so far?

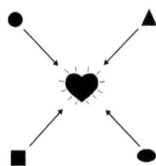

What do you wish was true for you here?
What is your 'Ah-Ha' moment here?

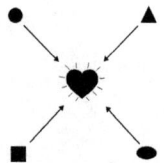

Are there things you need to do differently?
What are they, and what are three things you can do to make them happen?

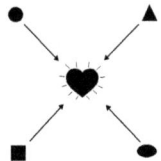

Other thoughts?

8

In every situation we can choose to feel better or to feel worse.

– Esther Hicks

Will you choose to feel better or worse?

In every aspect of your life you have choices. In every situation, and in every second, you can choose your life direction and the ways in which you will experience the life lessons that come to you. In every moment you can choose to be conscious or unconscious in your connection.

You can choose to get caught in a spiral of negativity and loss of control, or you can step into your power and understand the lesson in front of you. You can be overcome by illness or you can move forwards in good health.

You have control. You have power. You have choice. The question is this: will you choose to feel better or worse?

What were your first thoughts when reading this quote and considering this question?
How did the question and quote make you feel?
Where has this shown up as a pattern in your life?

How are you grateful for your experience with this so far?

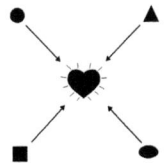

What do you wish was true for you here?
What is your 'Ah-Ha' moment here?

Are there things you need to do differently?
What are they, and what are three things you can do to make them happen?

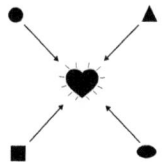

Other thoughts?

9

'I AM' are two of the most powerful words we ever use, for what you put after them shapes your reality.

– Anonymous

What words will you place after 'I AM' today?

I AM. Two little words … with SO MUCH POWER. You probably weren't taught about their significance in your life. That's okay; you're coming to understand them now. I AM shapes who you are – the words connect directly to the energetic source of the Universe. Using those two words together provides direction to the world around you.

When you use them, you are instructing the Universe in what it is you want to have provided. So be conscious – be connected – with the words you use after I AM, for what you put after them is what your reality will become.

What were your first thoughts when reading this quote and considering this question?
How did the question and quote make you feel?
Where has this shown up as a pattern in your life?

How are you grateful for your experience with this so far?

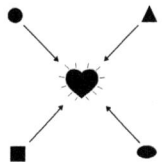

What do you wish was true for you here?
What is your 'Ah-Ha' moment here?

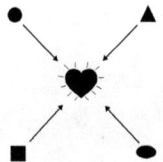

Are there things you need to do differently?
What are they, and what are three things you can do to make them happen?

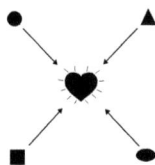

Other thoughts?

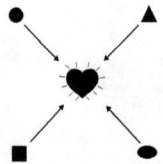

10

Where will your imagination take you?

– Bronwen Sciortino

Where will your imagination take you?

Can you imagine? That question is asked often, usually when someone is trying to get you to grasp the gravity of a situation. This question is one that is guaranteed to make you feel – and at a depth that it is hard for you to get to on your own. So why not use it to fuel your intentions?

Why not use it to broaden your mind and start to get curious about where you can go? Let your imagination run free and then watch with curiosity the way your life unfolds.

What were your first thoughts when reading this quote and considering this question?
How did the question and quote make you feel?
Where has this shown up as a pattern in your life?

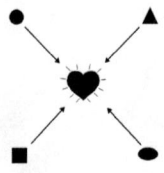

How are you grateful for your experience with this so far?

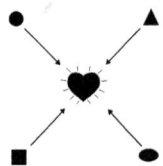

What do you wish was true for you here?
What is your 'Ah-Ha' moment here?

Are there things you need to do differently?
What are they, and what are three things you can do to make them happen?

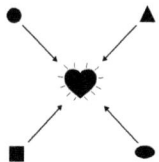

Other thoughts?

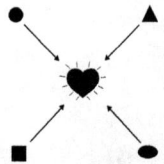

11

Be fearless in the pursuit of what sets your soul on fire.

– Anonymous

What sets your soul on fire?

Do you know the things that make your heart sing? The things that make your eyes light up and your soul want to get there and be there right now? Are they people? Places? Objects? Things? What do you feel when you're around them? What do they give to you and what happens to your energy?

Identify them and then find a way you can have them more often in your life … because when your soul is on fire, your heart is alive, and the world will always be a brighter and more colourful place.

What were your first thoughts when reading this quote and considering this question?

How did the question and quote make you feel?

Where has this shown up as a pattern in your life?

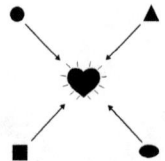

How are you grateful for your experience with this so far?

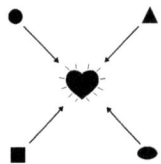

What do you wish was true for you here?
What is your 'Ah-Ha' moment here?

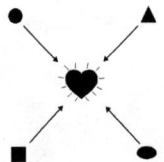

Are there things you need to do differently?
What are they, and what are three things you can do to make them happen?

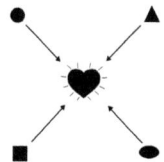

Other thoughts?

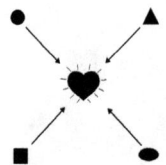

12

What if they're wrong?

– Gregg Braden

What if they're wrong?

From a very young age you were taught by the world around you what was good and bad, right and wrong, acceptable and not. As you learned, you carved out pieces of yourself and hid them from the world … because others told you they weren't right. In the end, you presented to the world a shaped version of yourself that you thought would be acceptable.
But … 'What if they're wrong?'

What if the things you've been told aren't right for you – and those pieces of yourself that you've hidden from the world – are the things that can make you feel whole again? Learn to ask this question and you'll start to reconnect with your one true guiding light.

What were your first thoughts when reading this quote and considering this question?
How did the question and quote make you feel?
Where has this shown up as a pattern in your life?

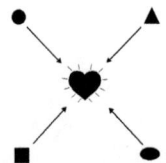

How are you grateful for your experience with this so far?

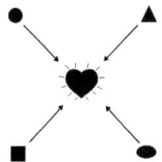

What do you wish was true for you here?
What is your 'Ah-Ha' moment here?

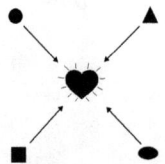

Are there things you need to do differently?
What are they, and what are three things you can do to make them happen?

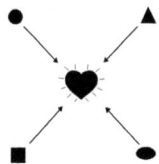

Other thoughts?

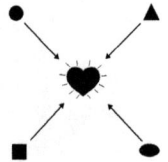

13

Master the power of a 'full stop' and you will hand yourself the keys to your freedom.

– Bronwen Sciortino

How will you use a 'full stop' to empower yourself today?

You've been taught to judge everyone around you as a way of determining where you are at in your life, your level of success and your level of worthiness. This creates an environment where you have to defend everything you are doing ... or might want to do.

By mastering the power of a 'full stop' you can step into an environment where you can simply state what you are doing – without any judgement or any need to defend your actions. A 'full stop' gives you the freedom to move your life in the way that works for you, without any restrictions or any need to make others see the worth of what you are doing.

What were your first thoughts when reading this quote and considering this question?
How did the question and quote make you feel?
Where has this shown up as a pattern in your life?

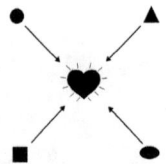

How are you grateful for your experience with this so far?

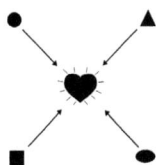

What do you wish was true for you here?
What is your 'Ah-Ha' moment here?

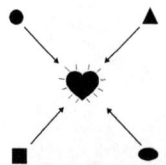

Are there things you need to do differently?
What are they, and what are three things you can do to make them happen?

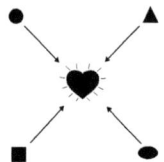

Other thoughts?

14

*If you had a friend who spoke to you the way you speak to yourself,
how long would you allow that person to remain as your friend?*

– Anonymous

How will you speak to yourself today?

From an early age you were taught that to believe in yourself or have a high opinion of yourself was wrong. If you showed any signs of having self-love or self-compassion, then you must have been 'on yourself' or 'up yourself'. Often this conditioning has been so strongly delivered that it can shape the voice inside you to become negatively focused.

When pointed at yourself, this voice can be vicious and mean, whilst being loving and empathetic when focused on someone else. Consider this: if you spoke to your friends the way you speak to yourself, how long would they keep you as their friend?

What were your first thoughts when reading this quote and considering this question?
How did the question and quote make you feel?
Where has this shown up as a pattern in your life?

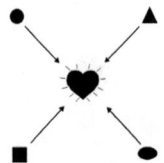

How are you grateful for your experience with this so far?

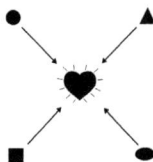

What do you wish was true for you here?
What is your 'Ah-Ha' moment here?

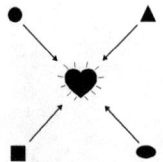

Are there things you need to do differently?
What are they, and what are three things you can do to make them happen?

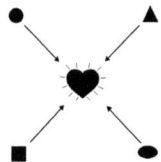

Other thoughts?

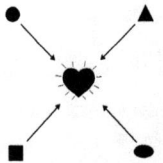

15

Kintsukuroi – the Japanese art of repairing pottery with gold or silver lacquer and understanding that the piece is more beautiful for having been broken.

– Anonymous

Which part of yourself is more beautiful for having been broken?

Chances are you've had multiple occasions throughout your life that have hurt you, where situations and/or people's actions have wounded your heart and it's felt like you've been broken. You can go through life carrying these wounds, or you can allow yourself to mend by fusing your pieces together with the understanding that your experiences have made your soul so much more beautiful.

Creating a Kintsukuroi process for yourself is the key to repairing those parts of yourself that you have always believed were broken. What once was broken can become whole again through the simple act of seeing the beauty within yourself.

What were your first thoughts when reading this quote and considering this question?
How did the question and quote make you feel?
Where has this shown up as a pattern in your life?

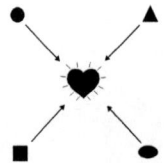

How are you grateful for your experience with this so far?

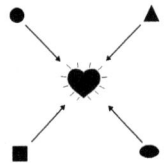

What do you wish was true for you here?
What is your 'Ah-Ha' moment here?

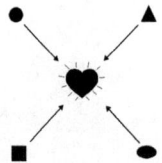

Are there things you need to do differently?
What are they, and what are three things you can do to make them happen?

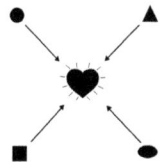

Other thoughts?

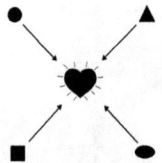

16

What will you do today to live daringly, boldly and fearlessly?

– Anonymous

What will you do today to live daringly, boldly and fearlessly?

Life can seem merciless in its ability to test you at every turn. Sometimes it feels like you've just got through one thing and it's already throwing the next challenge your way. It can be easy to fall into a routine that keeps you stuck, stumbling from one crisis to the next.

All it takes to do things a little bit differently is to identify something you really want to do and just one simple step you can take to start working towards having it. Call it courage, call it being bold, call it being fearless … call it whatever you want. Just take that one step and watch your life unfold in a different way.

What were your first thoughts when reading this quote and considering this question?
How did the question and quote make you feel?
Where has this shown up as a pattern in your life?

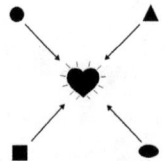

How are you grateful for your experience with this so far?

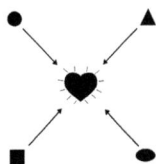

What do you wish was true for you here?
What is your 'Ah-Ha' moment here?

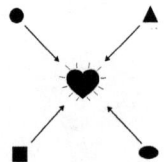

Are there things you need to do differently?
What are they, and what are three things you can do to make them happen?

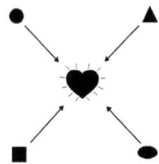

Other thoughts?

17

Will today be full of abundance … or will you fight tooth and nail for everything you can get?

– Bronwen Sciortino

How will you see the abundance in your life today?

You have been granted the gift of life. There are so many things you already have, yet you're distracted by the things that are yet to be in your possession. Clever marketers, aided by billions of dollars of research, have trained you to chase after the next material thing to fill the void in your life. You already have abundance – you simply don't realise that you've been trained to chase more.

Will you soften into the abundance that is already present, or will you chase and fight against the world for everything you can get?

What were your first thoughts when reading this quote and considering this question?
How did the question and quote make you feel?
Where has this shown up as a pattern in your life?

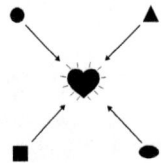

How are you grateful for your experience with this so far?

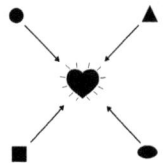

What do you wish was true for you here?
What is your 'Ah-Ha' moment here?

Are there things you need to do differently?
What are they, and what are three things you can do to make them happen?

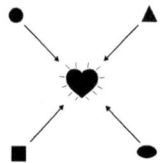

Other thoughts?

18

The more you are motivated by love,
the more fearless and free your action will be.

– The Dalai Lama

How will love motivate your today?

Every society, religion, group and community has standards that are deemed to be appropriate. If you step outside these standards, then you're looked at with disapproval. But you're unique – you are divinely different in your own special way. There isn't one set of rules that applies to every single individual in the Universe.

Your path forwards is paved with love. Allowing others to be their own selves does not affect your ability to stand in your truth. Will you walk that path with acceptance and tolerance, and allow every unique individual their divine right to be who they are – without judgement?

What were your first thoughts when reading this quote and considering this question?
How did the question and quote make you feel?
Where has this shown up as a pattern in your life?

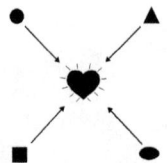

How are you grateful for your experience with this so far?

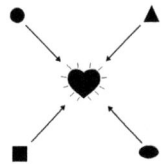

What do you wish was true for you here?
What is your 'Ah-Ha' moment here?

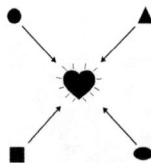

Are there things you need to do differently?
What are they, and what are three things you can do to make them happen?

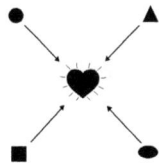

Other thoughts?

19

We often set out to make a difference in the life of others, only to discover that we have made a difference in our own.

– Ellie Braun-Haley

How will you make a difference in your life today?

You focus on doing things for others – on always being there when you are needed. Often, life gifts us the opportunity to do for ourselves as lovingly as we would do for others.

What do you need to give to yourself right now? How will you place a value and an importance on this? What will you do that will make a difference for you?

What were your first thoughts when reading this quote and considering this question?
How did the question and quote make you feel?
Where has this shown up as a pattern in your life?

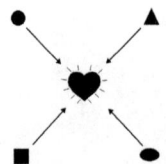

How are you grateful for your experience with this so far?

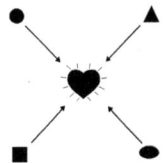

What do you wish was true for you here?
What is your 'Ah-Ha' moment here?

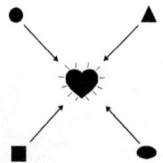

Are there things you need to do differently?
What are they, and what are three things you can do to make them happen?

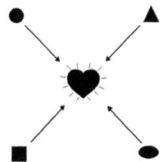

Other thoughts?

20

One's philosophy is not best expressed in words; it is expressed in the choices one makes … and the choices we make are ultimately our responsibility.

– Eleanor Roosevelt

What choices will you make today?

Life doesn't happen to you, it happens because of you. It is always your choices that create the life you experience. If someone does something that makes you unhappy, they aren't doing something to you, but rather they are a mirror reflecting back to you something for you to learn.

Your life is yours. You are not responsible for someone else's behaviour, but you are absolutely responsible for yours. There are choices in every situation. What choices will you make today to take responsibility for your life?

What were your first thoughts when reading this quote and considering this question?
How did the question and quote make you feel?
Where has this shown up as a pattern in your life?

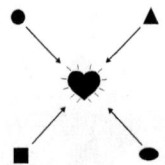

How are you grateful for your experience with this so far?

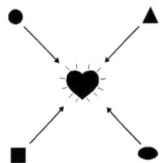

What do you wish was true for you here?
What is your 'Ah-Ha' moment here?

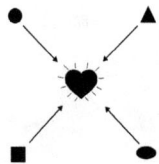

Are there things you need to do differently?
What are they, and what are three things you can do to make them happen?

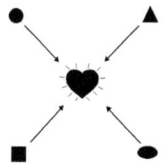

Other thoughts?

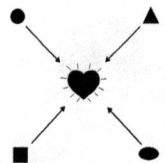

21

Do what feels right for you.
You must listen to the whisper which is heard by you alone.

– Ralph Waldo Emerson

What is YOUR whisper telling you today?

You know it – that voice that whispers in your head. You know when something is right, just as you know when something is wrong. How many times have you settled for something, or stepped into doing something, when you've known it's not right for you?

Why do you do it anyway? Focus on the whisper. Take notice of what it is telling you – asking of you. Follow its lead and see where you belong.

What were your first thoughts when reading this quote and considering this question?

How did the question and quote make you feel?

Where has this shown up as a pattern in your life?

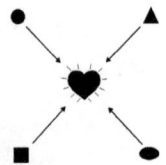

How are you grateful for your experience with this so far?

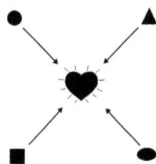

What do you wish was true for you here?
What is your 'Ah-Ha' moment here?

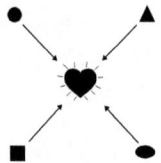

Are there things you need to do differently?
What are they, and what are three things you can do to make them happen?

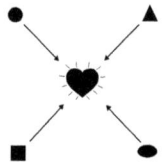

Other thoughts?

22

Chance is always powerful. Let your hook always be cast in the pool where you least expect there will be fish.

– Ovid

What chances will you take today?

Sometimes in life an opportunity comes along and it requires you to take what feels like a massive step to be able to harness it. It is in these moments that your greatest opportunity for growth exists. Life will always grace you with steps – sometimes they're big, sometimes they're small, and they can be in any direction.

It's the steps that make your stomach churn – the ones that require you to take a massive breath, close your eyes and jump – that will be the difference in your life. Will you step up and take them?

What were your first thoughts when reading this quote and considering this question?
How did the question and quote make you feel?
Where has this shown up as a pattern in your life?

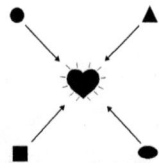

How are you grateful for your experience with this so far?

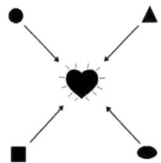

What do you wish was true for you here?
What is your 'Ah-Ha' moment here?

Are there things you need to do differently?
What are they, and what are three things you can do to make them happen?

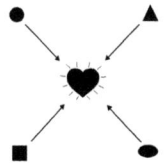

Other thoughts?

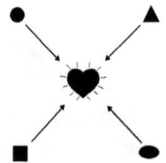

23

What can you do today to trust that you are exactly where you are meant to be?

Life can be tumultuous … not knowing where you're at, what you're supposed to be doing or why you keep having such a tough time. If you get caught in a spiral of doubt, it can seem like you're in a pressure cooker, like you're being hit from every direction all at once.

One of the easiest pathways out of this spiral is to stop and find the common thread between the challenges. The theme of the thread will be where your lesson lies. Once you can see the thread you'll know where to better focus your attention.

What were your first thoughts when reading this quote and considering this question?
How did the question and quote make you feel?
Where has this shown up as a pattern in your life?

How are you grateful for your experience with this so far?

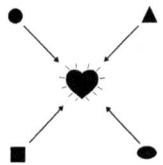

What do you wish was true for you here?
What is your 'Ah-Ha' moment here?

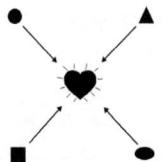

Are there things you need to do differently?
What are they, and what are three things you can do to make them happen?

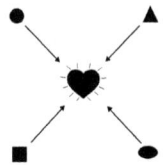

Other thoughts?

24

You are free when you can be yourself no matter what is happening around you.

– Bronwen Sciortino

How will you be free today?

Do you have places, people and situations in your life where you feel like you can't be yourself? What, where or who are they? What do they have in common? What happens when you are in these situations? How do you feel when you're in or around them?

These questions will help to give you the freedom to explore who you become, and the things that are holding you back in those situations.

What were your first thoughts when reading this quote and considering this question?
How did the question and quote make you feel?
Where has this shown up as a pattern in your life?

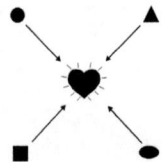

How are you grateful for your experience with this so far?

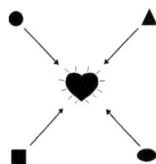

What do you wish was true for you here?
What is your 'Ah-Ha' moment here?

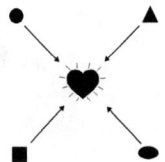

Are there things you need to do differently?
What are they, and what are three things you can do to make them happen?

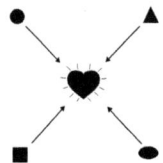

Other thoughts?

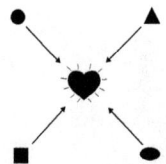

25

The depth of your greatness will shine through every time you let it.

– Bronwen Sciortino

How will you let yourself shine today?

You are a unique individual. There is no one else in the Universe who is like you. You have a greatness that cannot be replicated, no matter how hard another may try. When you hide your greatness from the world, you make it harder for the world to be whole.

The only time your greatness is hidden is when you actively work to hide it from the world. When you step out of the way and allow yourself to be seen, the world lights up and everyone benefits. Without you, the world is fractured. With you, the world cannot help but shine.

What were your first thoughts when reading this quote and considering this question?

How did the question and quote make you feel?

Where has this shown up as a pattern in your life?

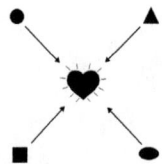

How are you grateful for your experience with this so far?

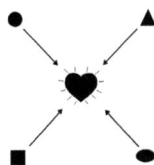

What do you wish was true for you here?
What is your 'Ah-Ha' moment here?

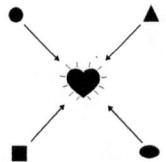

Are there things you need to do differently?
What are they, and what are three things you can do to make them happen?

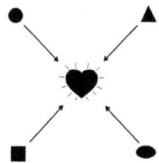

Other thoughts?

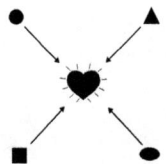

26

Growth happens when you make a decision to do something differently.

– Bronwen Sciortino

What will you do differently today?

While ever you sit in the same patterns in your life, doing and thinking the same things, your life will stagnate. You cannot move forward until you take a step to do something differently.

Every single time you take a step you create a change in your frequency. A frequency change provides an opportunity to grow. It doesn't matter what size the step is, nor the direction it takes. What matters is taking the step.

What were your first thoughts when reading this quote and considering this question?

How did the question and quote make you feel?

Where has this shown up as a pattern in your life?

How are you grateful for your experience with this so far?

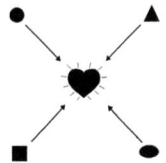

What do you wish was true for you here?
What is your 'Ah-Ha' moment here?

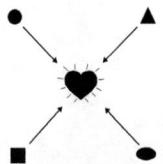

Are there things you need to do differently?
What are they, and what are three things you can do to make them happen?

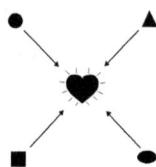

Other thoughts?

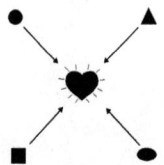

27

Our days are happier when we give people a bit of our heart rather than a piece of our mind.

– David Wolfe

How will you share your heart with people today?

As life gets more difficult, and you become more stressed and tired, it can seem like you need to protect yourself from the world. When you step into this way of being, it becomes normal to judge the behaviour of others and to tell them what they're doing wrong, instead of giving them kindness and compassion to allow them to grow.

Imagine, if instead of boxing yourself away from the world so you don't have to solve everyone's problems, you could simply send them thoughts of kindness and love to help them through their day. The energy you consume to do this is less, and the energy exchange they receive is greater. That's always going to be a win-win.

What were your first thoughts when reading this quote and considering this question?
How did the question and quote make you feel?
Where has this shown up as a pattern in your life?

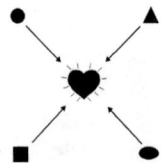

How are you grateful for your experience with this so far?

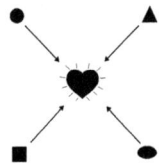

What do you wish was true for you here?
What is your 'Ah-Ha' moment here?

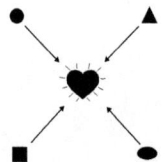

Are there things you need to do differently?
What are they, and what are three things you can do to make them happen?

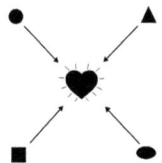

Other thoughts?

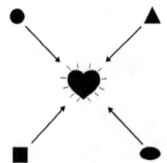

28

What you do right now is a part of your legacy.
What will you leave behind?

– Bronwen Sciortino

What will you leave behind today?

Everything you do is a part of the history you create. You've been taught to look to great people from history for your inspiration, but history is made by every living soul. You leave an energetic imprint in every moment.

Every energetic imprint codes the future for generations to come. What you do matters – in every moment. What will your legacy be? What will you leave behind?

What were your first thoughts when reading this quote and considering this question?

How did the question and quote make you feel?

Where has this shown up as a pattern in your life?

How are you grateful for your experience with this so far?

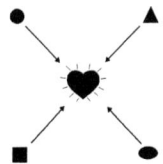

What do you wish was true for you here?
What is your 'Ah-Ha' moment here?

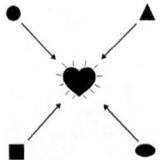

Are there things you need to do differently?
What are they, and what are three things you can do to make them happen?

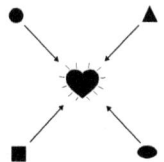

Other thoughts?

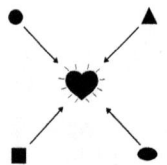

29

What if being YOU is the quickest path to happiness?

– Bronwen Sciortino

How will you be YOU today?

There are so many ways in which you're told who you should be, and how you should be doing things. There's a multi-billion-dollar marketing industry that is designed specifically to hit your trigger points and make you as malleable as possible.

Standing tall against this can be difficult if you're unaware that it exists. It's time to consciously connect with who you truly are. Who are you? What do you stand for? What's important to you? Start with these questions and then see what feels out of alignment within your life.

What were your first thoughts when reading this quote and considering this question?

How did the question and quote make you feel?

Where has this shown up as a pattern in your life?

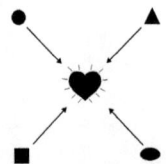

How are you grateful for your experience with this so far?

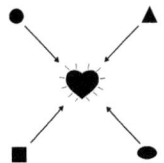

What do you wish was true for you here?
What is your 'Ah-Ha' moment here?

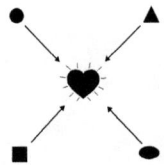

Are there things you need to do differently?
What are they, and what are three things you can do to make them happen?

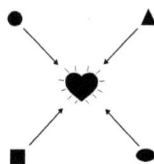

Other thoughts?

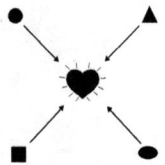

30

If you are always racing to the next moment,
what happens to the one you're in?

– Anonymous

What will you do to make sure you enjoy each moment of your day?

Do you spend a lot of time worrying about something that has happened in the past? Or trying to work out what might happen in the future? The past is known and provides a great platform for learning. The future is yours for the making.

But this moment – right now – is the moment that counts. The gold in this moment creates gratitude and wonder and sparks your creativity. If you let the gold go and ignore the present, then you limit your ability to stand in your true potential.

What were your first thoughts when reading this quote and considering this question?
How did the question and quote make you feel?
Where has this shown up as a pattern in your life?

How are you grateful for your experience with this so far?

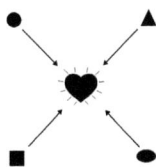

What do you wish was true for you here?
What is your 'Ah-Ha' moment here?

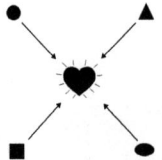

Are there things you need to do differently?
What are they, and what are three things you can do to make them happen?

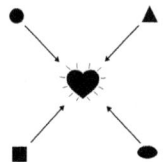

Other thoughts?

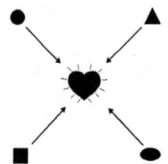

31

When you talk, you are only repeating what you already know.
But if you listen, you may learn something new.

– The Dalai Lama

What will you learn today?

When you go to school the system tells you that you're either a good or bad student. But there are so many ways for you to truly learn. Learning is not about sitting within a system of judgement imposed on you by others.

It's about moving towards the things that interest you and listening to see what you can absorb. What are you passionate about? What catches your eye and holds your interest? What does your soul yearn to know more about?

What were your first thoughts when reading this quote and considering this question?

How did the question and quote make you feel?

Where has this shown up as a pattern in your life?

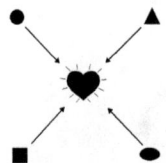

How are you grateful for your experience with this so far?

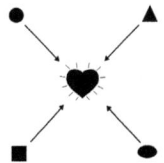

What do you wish was true for you here?
What is your 'Ah-Ha' moment here?

Are there things you need to do differently?
What are they, and what are three things you can do to make them happen?

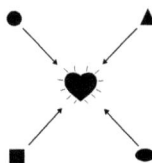

Other thoughts?

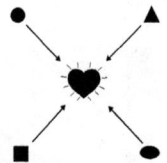

32

Time is a created thing. To say 'I don't have time,'
is like saying 'I don't want to'.

– Lao Tzu

How will you use time to your advantage today?

Being stuck in time is one of the greatest distractions of life.
The faster life gets, the less it seems like you have the time you need to
get everything done. But time is relative.

Enough time for one person is nowhere near enough time for you. What if
you could take time out of the equation? What would happen to the way
you approach your day? How can you step outside the influence that time
has and create a new paradigm for your life?

What were your first thoughts when reading this quote and considering this question?

How did the question and quote make you feel?

Where has this shown up as a pattern in your life?

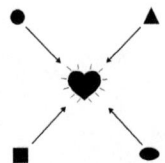

How are you grateful for your experience with this so far?

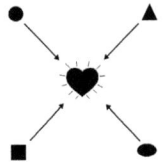

What do you wish was true for you here?
What is your 'Ah-Ha' moment here?

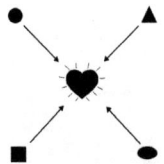

Are there things you need to do differently?
What are they, and what are three things you can do to make them happen?

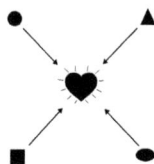

Other thoughts?

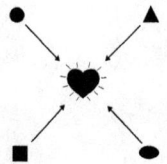

33

You're stressed and exhausted … what do you need to change?

– Bronwen Sciortino

What do you need to change?

When you let stress take hold of you it can be hard to break free. If you allow stress to run wild, then before you know it your body becomes addicted to the hormone cocktail that stress creates, and you can find yourself subconsciously creating stressful moments so that your body can feed its addiction.

Take a moment to connect with yourself and discover where your stress is coming from. Is it feeding your exhaustion? If your answer to this question is 'yes' then it might be time for you to find one thing that you can do differently so you can lessen the hold that stress has in your life.

What were your first thoughts when reading this quote and considering this question?
How did the question and quote make you feel?
Where has this shown up as a pattern in your life?

How are you grateful for your experience with this so far?

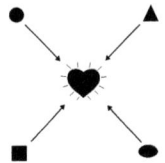

What do you wish was true for you here?
What is your 'Ah-Ha' moment here?

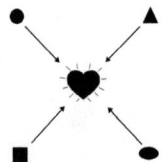

Are there things you need to do differently?
What are they, and what are three things you can do to make them happen?

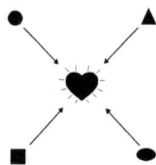

Other thoughts?

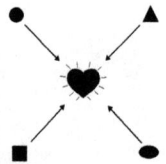

34

No matter how long you've travelled in the wrong direction ...
you can always turn around.

– Anonymous

What will you turn around today?

There are so many times in your life that you turn to a GPS to help navigate to your next destination. No matter how many times you deviate from the path it lays out for you, it will recalculate and create a new path for you. The same is true for your life.

It doesn't matter where you are starting from, or how many detours you take along the way, it is movement that will keep you going. So choose something you want and then find just one step to help you get there. If that step takes you in a direction that you weren't expecting, that's fine – simply decide on the next step and the next until you end up where you want to go.

What were your first thoughts when reading this quote and considering this question?
How did the question and quote make you feel?
Where has this shown up as a pattern in your life?

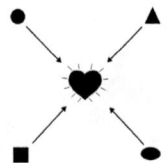

How are you grateful for your experience with this so far?

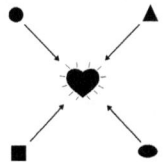

What do you wish was true for you here?
What is your 'Ah-Ha' moment here?

Are there things you need to do differently?
What are they, and what are three things you can do to make them happen?

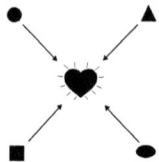

Other thoughts?

35

Don't walk behind me; I may not lead. Don't walk in front of me; I may not follow. Just walk beside me and be my friend.

– Winnie the Pooh

Where will you walk today?

As long as you keep your focus on following the footsteps or directions that someone else gives you, you will have no control over where you end up, nor whether you are heading in a direction that is right for you. There will always be people around you that are happy to tell you what you should and shouldn't be doing. But the only person who truly knows what is right for you is YOU.

By all means, find quality people who will walk with you on your journey ... but always make your own decisions about which direction you will go and how you will get to where you are going.

What were your first thoughts when reading this quote and considering this question?
How did the question and quote make you feel?
Where has this shown up as a pattern in your life?

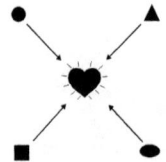

How are you grateful for your experience with this so far?

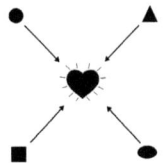

What do you wish was true for you here?
What is your 'Ah-Ha' moment here?

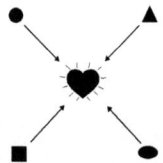

Are there things you need to do differently?
What are they, and what are three things you can do to make them happen?

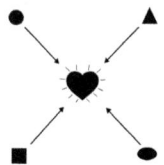

Other thoughts?

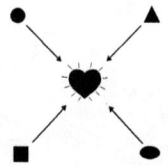

36

What people in the world think of you is none of your business.

– Martha Graham

How will you honour your opinion of yourself today?

You've been taught to hang on the words of others to find your direction in life ... but their opinion is based entirely on their experience of the world; it might not be relevant to you.

Who you listen to, and how you let what they say affect your life, is completely up to you. Find your connection to yourself, understand what is important to you and be guided by YOUR values to determine whether what is being said to you is relevant information for YOUR journey forwards.

What were your first thoughts when reading this quote and considering this question?
How did the question and quote make you feel?
Where has this shown up as a pattern in your life?

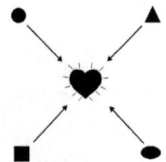

How are you grateful for your experience with this so far?

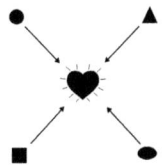

What do you wish was true for you here?
What is your 'Ah-Ha' moment here?

Are there things you need to do differently?
What are they, and what are three things you can do to make them happen?

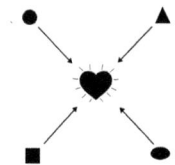

Other thoughts?

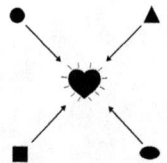

37

Everything you want is on the other side of fear.

– George Addair

What fear will you step into today?

From a very young age you were conditioned with all the things you shouldn't do because something would happen to you. Some of those things may well save your life – things like 'don't run out in front of a car'. Others are simply creating a box for you to sit in that is stopping you from reaching your true potential.

What are you afraid of? What holds you back? Pick one fear that you'd like to be free from and then find one simple step that allows you to walk away from its control in your life.

What were your first thoughts when reading this quote and considering this question?
How did the question and quote make you feel?
Where has this shown up as a pattern in your life?

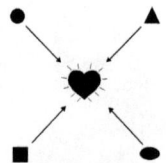

How are you grateful for your experience with this so far?

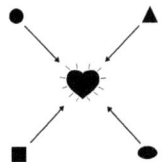

What do you wish was true for you here?
What is your 'Ah-Ha' moment here?

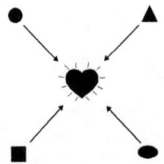

Are there things you need to do differently?
What are they, and what are three things you can do to make them happen?

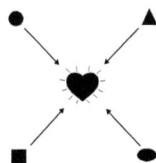

Other thoughts?

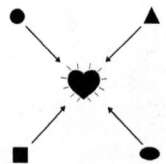

38

In a world focused on hate, fear and greed, how will you make sure you can love?

– Bronwen Sciortino

How can you make sure love is infused in everything you do today?

You've been taught to judge others as a way to determine where you are at in comparison. Why is there a need to determine whether someone else's behaviour is right or wrong?

Behind every action is a human being. It is the actions that we should review – not the person – for alignment with our I AM and I AM NOT characteristics. The actions provide us with a reflected image from which we can learn. Looking beyond the action and seeing the human being with eyes of love can make it easier for you to view the world in a simpler way.

What were your first thoughts when reading this quote and considering this question?
How did the question and quote make you feel?
Where has this shown up as a pattern in your life?

How are you grateful for your experience with this so far?

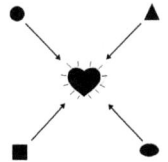

What do you wish was true for you here?
What is your 'Ah-Ha' moment here?

Are there things you need to do differently?
What are they, and what are three things you can do to make them happen?

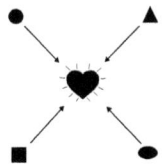

Other thoughts?

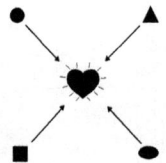

39

What mark will you leave on the world around you?

– Bronwen Sciortino

How will people feel after interacting with you today?

Everything you do, everything you say, every interaction you have with someone leaves a mark. When you are mean it is felt. When you are loving it is felt. Every feeling codes the energy of the Universe.

What you do directly touches the world. So, what mark do you want to leave on the world? What do you want people to feel after every interaction with you? What are you prepared to do to make sure this happens?

What were your first thoughts when reading this quote and considering this question?
How did the question and quote make you feel?
Where has this shown up as a pattern in your life?

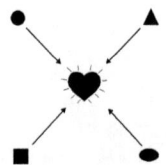

How are you grateful for your experience with this so far?

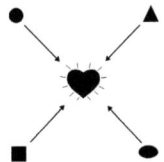

What do you wish was true for you here?
What is your 'Ah-Ha' moment here?

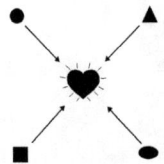

Are there things you need to do differently?
What are they, and what are three things you can do to make them happen?

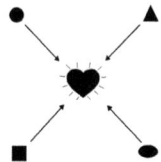

Other thoughts?

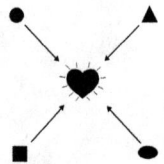

40

Happiness is only fleeting if you rely on it coming from someone else.

– Bronwen Sciortino

What makes you happy?

Happiness is one of the things that you crave the most, but with the speed of life and the pressure it brings, it can seem like you can either be successful or you can be happy. Happiness comes from within. It comes when you make a decision to be happy – no matter where you are or what you are doing. It relies on nothing other than your ability to love exactly where you are in every moment.

What are you grateful for? What are the things in your life that make your heart sing? Where do your moments of joy come from?

What were your first thoughts when reading this quote and considering this question?
How did the question and quote make you feel?
Where has this shown up as a pattern in your life?

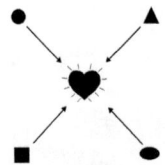

How are you grateful for your experience with this so far?

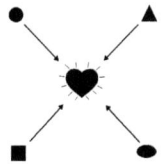

What do you wish was true for you here?
What is your 'Ah-Ha' moment here?

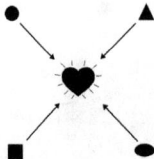

Are there things you need to do differently?
What are they, and what are three things you can do to make them happen?

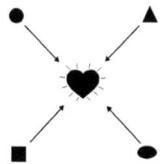

Other thoughts?

41

Just. Be. Kind.

– Bronwen Sciortino

How will kindness rule your day?

In a world where we are taught to judge so that we can determine where we are at in the world, kindness can often get lost.

When we use kindness and love as our FIRST filter it completely changes the way we view the world around us, and the people within it. It also allows us to open our hearts and our minds to the endless possibilities that come when we see the colour in the world. Bring kindness to the fore and you can change your perspective on everything.

What were your first thoughts when reading this quote and considering this question?
How did the question and quote make you feel?
Where has this shown up as a pattern in your life?

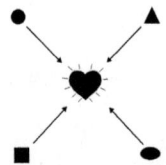

How are you grateful for your experience with this so far?

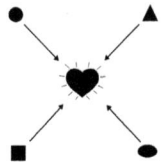

What do you wish was true for you here?
What is your 'Ah-Ha' moment here?

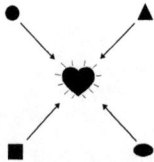

Are there things you need to do differently?
What are they, and what are three things you can do to make them happen?

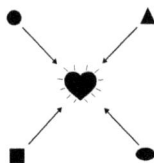

Other thoughts?

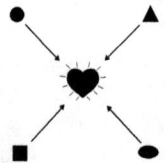

42

Your inner knowledge – your intuition –
is always the best compass for YOUR life.

– Bronwen Sciortino

How will you trust your intuition and follow where it leads you today?

When you were a child, you probably answered a question with 'I just know'. It didn't matter whether someone else believed you; it was enough that you knew. Then somewhere along the way you started believing that other people held the key to your answers, and you turned away from your inner knowing - your intuition.

It's time to release the ties that bind your inner guidance and trust that you are the best guide to move the direction of your life. No one knows you better than you … why would you allow someone else to make your important decisions?

What were your first thoughts when reading this quote and considering this question?
How did the question and quote make you feel?
Where has this shown up as a pattern in your life?

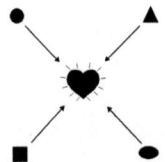

How are you grateful for your experience with this so far?

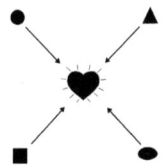

What do you wish was true for you here?
What is your 'Ah-Ha' moment here?

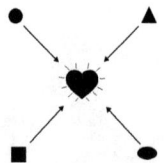

Are there things you need to do differently?
What are they, and what are three things you can do to make them happen?

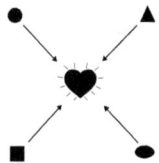

Other thoughts?

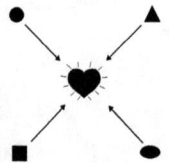

43

If there was one thing you could stop doing or being involved in right now ...
what would it be?

– Bronwen Sciortino

Why wouldn't you do everything you can to make your life as wonderful as you can ... right now?

You often find yourself doing things, or spending time with people, when you really don't want to. Increasing your conscious awareness of these areas of your life enables you to identify and reduce their occurrence. Imagine if you could spend most of your time doing things, and being with people, that inspire and energise you.

Would your world be a wonderful place to wake up every day? Would you jump out of bed and race towards your day with enthusiasm and joy? If this is how you feel, then what are you waiting for? Why wouldn't you make it a priority to make that happen now?

What were your first thoughts when reading this quote and considering this question?
How did the question and quote make you feel?
Where has this shown up as a pattern in your life?

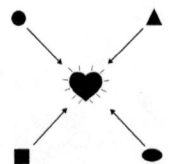

How are you grateful for your experience with this so far?

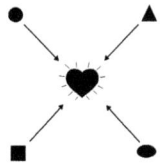

What do you wish was true for you here?
What is your 'Ah-Ha' moment here?

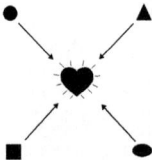

Are there things you need to do differently?
What are they, and what are three things you can do to make them happen?

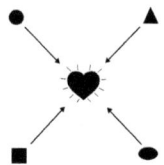

Other thoughts?

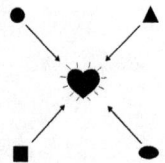

44

What would courage have me do today?

– Dr Libby Weaver

What is the one thing you will find the courage to do today?

Sometimes there's that one thing that you've been wanting or needing to do. It's been niggling at you for ages, but you find a way – any way – to have a million other more important things to do. Start by asking why you want or need it. Why is it important to you? What's stopping you from having it or doing it? Then take a deep breath, build the courage within yourself and create the action that allows you to take the step you need to go and do it.

Remember, the things that seem to need the most courage are often the things that allow your next spurt of growth. They're the things that make your life shine and allow you to change the direction you are heading.

So take the breath, grow the courage and take the action – it's always worth it in the end.

What were your first thoughts when reading this quote and considering this question?
How did the question and quote make you feel?
Where has this shown up as a pattern in your life?

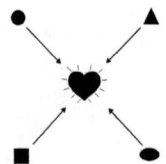

How are you grateful for your experience with this so far?

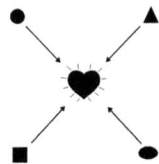

What do you wish was true for you here?
What is your 'Ah-Ha' moment here?

Are there things you need to do differently?
What are they, and what are three things you can do to make them happen?

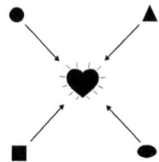

Other thoughts?

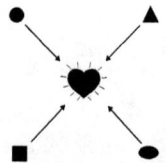

45

I was my own harshest critic and I had created such extreme expectations of myself that I had stacked my own game of life against me.

– Bronwen Sciortino

What expectations of yourself will you let go?

In life, you are often your own harshest critic. It can be hard for you to take a compliment, always turning someone's praise into another meaning or finding a way to minimise their words. Sometimes the biggest growth comes when you're able to acknowledge your strengths for yourself.

The moment when you give yourself a big compliment, one that is full of truth – that's the moment in time when you start to let the light back into your heart. When you allow yourself to feel the warmth of the glow within yourself you will truly be ready to walk your own way in the world.

What were your first thoughts when reading this quote and considering this question?
How did the question and quote make you feel?
Where has this shown up as a pattern in your life?

How are you grateful for your experience with this so far?

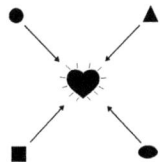

What do you wish was true for you here?
What is your 'Ah-Ha' moment here?

Are there things you need to do differently?
What are they, and what are three things you can do to make them happen?

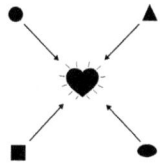

Other thoughts?

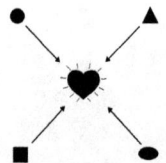

46

If you aren't grateful for what you already have, what makes you think you would be happy with more?

– Roy T. Bennett

What will you say thank you for today?

Life can get busy. You're often head down, trying to force each step to happen – just to make it through each day. Living like this creates pressure, and within that pressure it is easy to lose sight of everything that you have. It's time to raise your head and look up.

Remember all the fabulous things you have in your life and take a moment or two to be truly grateful for them. Never forget that if you have running water, food on the table, a roof over your head and electricity, you are wealthier than 85% of people on the planet.

What were your first thoughts when reading this quote and considering this question?
How did the question and quote make you feel?
Where has this shown up as a pattern in your life?

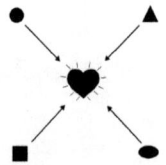

How are you grateful for your experience with this so far?

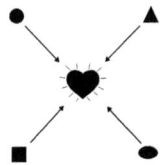

What do you wish was true for you here?
What is your 'Ah-Ha' moment here?

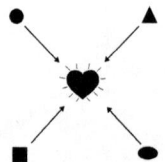

Are there things you need to do differently?
What are they, and what are three things you can do to make them happen?

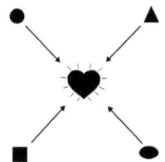

Other thoughts?

47

It's okay to take a rest.

– Bronwen Sciortino

How will you take a break today?

It can be easy to feel like taking a rest means quitting. Somehow, you've been taught that looking after yourself is selfish, or that stepping out of something you've been doing means letting others down. If you don't make sure you have what you need, for YOUR life, then you will find yourself with nothing left to give to others.

Refuel your energy tank first, align what you do for others with things that are important to you, and you will be more likely to have loads to give when others need you to lend a hand.

What were your first thoughts when reading this quote and considering this question?
How did the question and quote make you feel?
Where has this shown up as a pattern in your life?

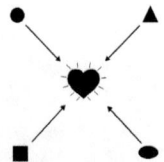

How are you grateful for your experience with this so far?

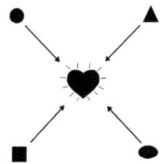

What do you wish was true for you here?
What is your 'Ah-Ha' moment here?

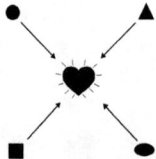

Are there things you need to do differently?
What are they, and what are three things you can do to make them happen?

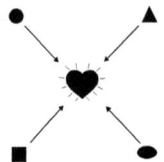

Other thoughts?

48

Give yourself the credit you are due.

– Bronwen Sciortino

What credit are you due?

Often, you're too scared to acknowledge the things that are amazing about yourself – the things that make you undeniably YOU. When you were young there were plenty of people around to 'bring you back to earth' if you strayed into 'loving yourself' territory.

There is nothing 'uppity' or 'on yourself' about knowing your strengths. There is only love and kindness in giving yourself the credit that you are due. Knowing who you are is the strongest platform you can build for your life. Who are you? What do you stand for? What credit are you due?

What were your first thoughts when reading this quote and considering this question?
How did the question and quote make you feel?
Where has this shown up as a pattern in your life?

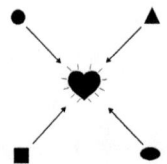

How are you grateful for your experience with this so far?

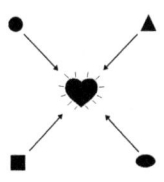

What do you wish was true for you here?
What is your 'Ah-Ha' moment here?

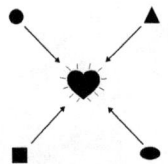

Are there things you need to do differently?
What are they, and what are three things you can do to make them happen?

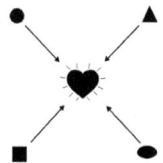

Other thoughts?

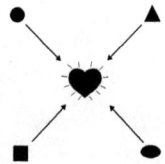

49

*Allow yourself a bit of time and space to simply **breathe**.*

– Bronwen Sciortino

How can you boost your energy today?

If you continuously push through the warning signs in your life, you'll likely find yourself on the way to collapsing.

There is a different way to live, and one of the best places to start is to make it a priority to give yourself things that help to boost your energy. What are the people, places and things that always make you feel great? How can you give yourself one of them each day?

What were your first thoughts when reading this quote and considering this question?

How did the question and quote make you feel?

Where has this shown up as a pattern in your life?

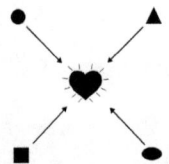

How are you grateful for your experience with this so far?

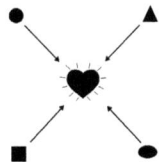

What do you wish was true for you here?
What is your 'Ah-Ha' moment here?

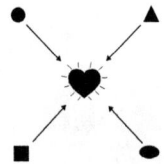

Are there things you need to do differently?
What are they, and what are three things you can do to make them happen?

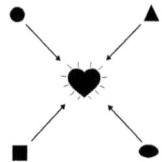

Other thoughts?

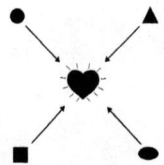

50

As long as I was searching externally for my answers,
I was always going to come up short.

– Bronwen Sciortino

What is right for you today?

Throughout life you're constantly told what you should and shouldn't do, how you should and shouldn't do it and with whom you should and shouldn't be doing it. Over time, you've spent so long following the directives of others that you have forgotten that you're the only one who KNOWS what it is you need.

The best way to work out what it is you need is to practice asking yourself questions before seeking answers from others. So, what is it you need right here, right now? How will you give that to yourself today?

What were your first thoughts when reading this quote and considering this question?

How did the question and quote make you feel?

Where has this shown up as a pattern in your life?

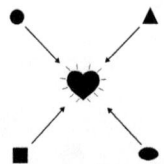

How are you grateful for your experience with this so far?

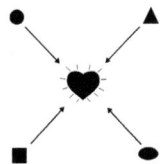

What do you wish was true for you here?
What is your 'Ah-Ha' moment here?

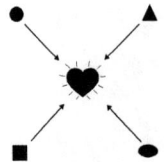

Are there things you need to do differently?
What are they, and what are three things you can do to make them happen?

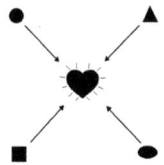

Other thoughts?

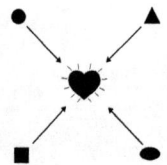

51

Don't make yourself small. Not for anyone.

– L.R. Knost

How will you live differently today?

You can leave change until the last minute – that minute when you're desolate, almost inconsolable and when the pain of your life is simply too much to bear. Or, you can acknowledge that the way you are living isn't working for you and you can choose to take a few small, simple steps to live your life in a different way.

Choose something you'd really like to have in your life and then take one step towards having it. Be more interested in how you can be the greatest version of yourself rather than being confined by the limits other people give you.

What were your first thoughts when reading this quote and considering this question?

How did the question and quote make you feel?

Where has this shown up as a pattern in your life?

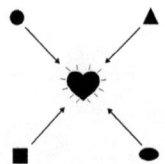

How are you grateful for your experience with this so far?

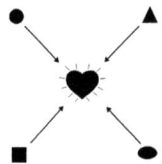

What do you wish was true for you here?
What is your 'Ah-Ha' moment here?

Are there things you need to do differently?
What are they, and what are three things you can do to make them happen?

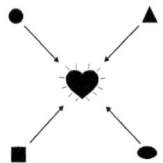

Other thoughts?

52

I reject your reality and substitute my own.

– Adam Savage

What rules will you break today?

In life, you're often held back by beliefs or conditioning that you've been given by other people. Your reality is shaped by how strongly you place yourself within the confines of the boundaries that you create for yourself.

To release yourself from these shackles, you need to let out your inner rebel and start to break all your rules. Start by choosing one rule that you've put in place for yourself and then work out one way to break that rule. Set yourself free by breaking each rule – one at a time!

What were your first thoughts when reading this quote and considering this question?
How did the question and quote make you feel?
Where has this shown up as a pattern in your life?

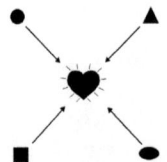

How are you grateful for your experience with this so far?

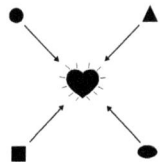

What do you wish was true for you here?
What is your 'Ah-Ha' moment here?

Are there things you need to do differently?
What are they, and what are three things you can do to make them happen?

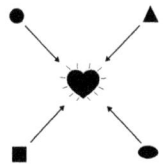

Other thoughts?

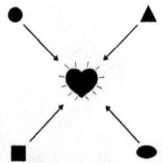

CONTACT DETAILS

To book Bronwen Sciortino for a keynote presentation, half or full day workshop nationally or internationally, please contact:

shelQ Life
PO Box 65
Melville, WA 6956
Australia

Ph: +61 438 624 868
E: info@sheiqlife.com
W: www.bronwensciortino.com

OTHER TITLES BY BRONWEN SCIORTINO

THE ECONOMY OF
ENOUGH

BRONWEN SCIORTINO

Never put off being kind to yourself again.

What if you could go from feeling like the worst person in the world to stepping into happily ever after?

How about in the time it takes you to read this book?

'You're useless....' 'You're so dumb...' 'How could you be so stupid?'
How many times have you said these things to yourself?

Probably multiple times a day, every day of your life, if this describes how you feel about yourself:

- Never have a kind word for yourself
- Easily find ways you could have done something better
- Have a foreboding sense of resignation that you'll never get anything 'right'
- Hold yourself to much higher standards than everyone else
- Nothing you ever do is 'good enough'

In her latest book, award-winning business woman Bronwen Sciortino unlocks the secret to happily ever after and shares practical and easy steps to allow you to experience the same love and commitment you give to everyone around you.

From exhausted to exulted, this book reveals just how easily you can infuse your life with outrageous happiness, love and laughter – using an easy to follow process and with loads of ease and grace.

The world is waiting for you to become the magnificent person you were always supposed to be.

Let's be real. There are no 'miracle' cures that work without applying attention. But there are simple and practical steps you can easily take to move your life in a different direction.

Infused with all the 'downloads' you need to catapult your life differently, The Economy of Enough is the golden nugget you've been waiting for to understand exactly what you need to be happy.

Keep It Super Simple

Reducing Stress and Increasing Resilience, a brilliant guide to overcoming overwhelm, 'Keep It Super Simple' is the book you didn't know you needed!

When it comes to creating a simpler life there's many things that can impact you. This highly engaging book by award-winning business woman and author, Bronwen Sciortino, offers a brilliantly simple approach to overcoming overwhelm and living a life with less stress and more resilience.

Described as 'chocolate for your soul' ... 'Keep It Super Simple' shows you how to:

- live life differently every day because in a world wher e you lead a life filled with stress and exhaustion, you're robbing yourself of a fulfilled, healthy and happier life;
- find the best ways to recharge YOUR energy so you can stop being exhausted all the time;
- understand the importance of creating your values, how to align your life to them & live every day being true to you so you can bring your life into flow, bringing an ease and effortlessness you'll absolutely love;
- minimise the impact of FOMO & YOLO on your life which means you consciously choose the things you love doing rather than spending your life doing the things others tell you that you 'should' be doing;
- create the simple and practical steps that help make sure you're doing the things that are aligned with who you are, replacing the time and energy you have been putting into trying to be someone or something else with more rewarding ways of living and being;
- step away from stress & live a life that is calm & full of energy;
- easily implement simple steps that empower you in YOUR life – leading you to experience greater confidence and self integrity;
- have the confidence that there IS light at the end of the tunnel and that you are not stuck living a life someone else has given you;
- be yourself whilst limiting the impact of shame, guilt & recriminations from others;
- understand YOUR path to success so you can boldly step into the thick of YOUR life;

This book easily fits in your bag so you can easily take it with you everywhere you go, which means it'll be there as a support anytime you need it; AND it's in a workbook style, offering space for journaling and recording your 'Ah-Ha' moments – deepening your understanding and ability to implement the new learning into your life. You can build on your thoughts, comments & feelings – almost like a diary which means you'll never lose the important nuggets that will help you to move forward in your life.

Don't be surprised when you turn this into a reference for every day situations – it's likely to become a reflection tool that teaches you to make your own choices and guide your life as you learn to find your path forward.

THANK YOU

There's a special journey with every book written, and this one was no different. I gained insights and again I was very privileged to have the words flow through me so freely. This book is offered back to the Universe with as much love as it was given to me.

Support in my everyday life makes it so easy for me to create. I am truly thankful for the ongoing and unlimited love, support and encouragement that I receive from so many avenues in my life:

- Jon Sciortino – as always, my unwavering # 1 fan – you're a constant voice of reason, encouraging where needed, challenging me when it's required and never failing to wax lyrical about me to anyone who will listen. I love that you're on this journey with me, and that there's a bit of you in every piece of work I send out into the world.

- My incomparably awesome friends – Sharon Marsden, Karen & Andre Clay, Catherine Rapley – wherever we are, the bonds of our friendship are unbreakable. I am truly blessed to have you as my friends – the Universe was kind to me the day it placed you in my life.

- Melaney Ryan – you continue to give to me with an incredible generosity. I am truly grateful to be learning from you, absorbing your wisdom and knowledge. Your unwavering belief in my ability to achieve my destiny in this lifetime is inspiring – I thank you from the bottom of my heart. Mahatma and so much love.

- Kelsey Allen – my typesetter extraordinaire and friend – thank you for the work you put into shaping the words into a visual masterpiece. I love that I get to work with you. Thank you for your ongoing support of all I do.

- Lorelei Ammon – the creator of the image on the cover – I cannot tell you how absolutely thrilled I was when the stars aligned and you were able to create a masterpiece that would fuel the essence of this book. It is so cool for me that we could collaborate and that you helped me to create the lasting image that will be carried into the world.

- Thank you to each and every one of my readers – your support over my journey, your words of love, testimonials, reviews and connection through the social media world mean so much to me.

Much love and may you all stand within the strength that comes from knowing exactly who you are.